Sexual
I·N·T·I·M·A·C·Y

And The Alcoholic Relationship

The Al-Anon Family Groups are a fellowship of relatives and friends of alcoholics who share their experience, strength and hope in order to solve their common problems. We believe alcoholism is a family illness and that changed attitudes can aid recovery.

Al-Anon is not allied with any sect, denomination, political entity, organization or institution; does not engage in any controversy, neither endorses nor opposes any cause. There are no dues for membership. Al-Anon is self-supporting through its own voluntary contributions.

Al-Anon has but one purpose: to help families of alcoholics. We do this by practicing the Twelve Steps, by welcoming and giving comfort to families of alcoholics, and by giving understanding and encouragement to the alcoholic.

–The Suggested Preamble to the Twelve Steps

For information and catalog of literature write:
AL-ANON FAMILY GROUP HEADQUARTERS, INC.
P.O. BOX 862, MIDTOWN STATION
NEW YORK, NEW YORK 10018-0862
212-302-7240
FAX 212-869-3757

AL-ANON FAMILY GROUP HEADQUARTERS, INC. 1993

ISBN 910034-87-7

Approved by
World Service Conference
Al-Anon Family Groups

1–30M–93–2.50   **P-77**   Printed in U.S.A.

CONTENTS

♦ ♦ ♦

I his booklet is a result of an Al-Anon member's plea for help. Her
question was in regard to sexual intimacy – and she was frustrated that the subject was rarely – if ever – addressed at Al-Anon
meetings. Through The FORUM, she requested thoughts from other
members on how one sustains an intimate relationship with an alcoholic partner.

For two years, members have been reaching out to her, sharing
through letters to The FORUM on their own experience with sexual intimacy. These letters (virtually all from women) are gathered together
here in hopes of providing gentle guidance to the question.

To some extent, these letters portray alcoholism as an obstacle to
sexual intimacy. But they also portray the obstacle being overcome.
There are stories of barriers breaking down, stories of trust starting to
develop, stories of people becoming closer to one another, sometimes
closer than ever before. Collectively, these sharings are a portrait of
pain, discovery, healing and growth. And they are proof – proof that
intimacy is possible – even within an actively alcoholic situation.

For many of us, the journey is just beginning. We hope this booklet
will inspire open-hearted discussion on forms of intimacy beyond the
sexual relationship: the closeness between parents and children, the
warmth between friends, the intimacy available to us in the opportunities we have to be vulnerable and touch one another, heart to heart.

♦ ♦ ♦

CHAPTER ONE

FEELING UNLOVED?

*S*exuality used to mean enjoyment for both of us — an experience to share. It was part of our being in love and an expression of our bond. Some time later, I knew that it had degenerated into revulsion and loathing.

From my own experience, however, this could be a part of the alcoholic's illness — in that desire increases while potency diminishes. We both became very frustrated. In addition, there was another problem which was more and more distressing — his personal hygiene. I did not know how often he washed himself or cleaned his teeth, which were rotted from drinking. I only knew that he stank when he got undressed.

I learned in Al-Anon that I certainly had the right to share my feelings with him. I waited one morning until he was awake, but not yet under the influence, in order to discuss things. He was furious and shouted at me to look for somebody else. I was completely devastated then. Nothing frightened me more than separation.

I could understand his anger, however — after all, no one likes to be told they are dirty. The second time we spoke about it, he was much quieter, and I was simply able to tell him he should shower before we made love. He understood this, and for awhile, things improved.

While taking the Fourth Step, I came across the questions as to whether I let my body be misused. This completely threw me. How often I had slept with him to avoid quarrels or his abuse! Then I started pleading tiredness and headaches as I did not have the courage to set boundaries. I put my own needs and feelings way behind his.

At the same time, I learned a lot in Al-Anon about letting go, and I understood it could not go on like this. Alcohol was always more important to him than me and so, eventually, I left him.

After the separation, I made an astonishing discovery — I could live without sex. I missed the tenderness and the caresses, so I had massages prescribed for me. I bought myself an electric blanket and enjoyed the warmth. My self-assurance improved knowing I was more or less able to manage on my own.

It was suddenly so much easier to be conscious of my needs and wishes, to take them seriously, and to fulfill them myself. My independence, my spiritual growth, the responsibility for my body's well-being — all of these I found I could take care of alone. Spiritual closeness has now become a prerequisite for physical closeness. It has never been my experience that out of physical closeness a spiritual closeness can arise, only vice-versa.

I now have a partner with whom I can talk. Trying to understand each other brings us nearer together. When there is a hitch with our sexual relationship, I have to start with myself. I have to take my own feelings seriously and listen to them. Only then can I make myself understood by another person.

♦ ♦ ♦

*T*here are a number of us who are dealing and coping with sex problems one day at a time.

Being in Al-Anon has helped me with my sexual problems. My husband is an active alcoholic and a paraplegic. I have accepted his disability; therefore my sexual goals are limited.

I have adjusted my mind and body to this. My spouse, however, being a young man, has not accepted anything. His male ego keeps him trying to prove himself. Problems: manhandling; constant petting; odor, sweat and lack of cleanliness due to drink; resentment; rejection; anger.

Recently I chose to chair a meeting on the chapter, "Sex in the Alcoholic Marriage" from the book, *The Dilemma of the Alcoholic Marriage*. I knew this was a serious problem for many. The turnout for this meeting was great. I put down some ground rules and had a list of questions I thought might be interesting:

- How do you say "no" with compassion?
- Do wives have rights?
- When does tenderness end and sexual abuse start?

These problems can be very serious. You see, I am a person who can be shown love in a number of ways other than sex — flowers, cards, communication, holding hands, or just a kiss — a simple kiss.

I have learned to say what I feel, stay with my decision and not feel guilty because of it.

The Al-Anon book, *The Dilemma of the Alcoholic Marriage*, and the AA Big Book, Chapter 5 "To the Wives," helped me understand my situation better. You can use the Twelve Steps in intimacy matters. You may need to!

◆ ◆ ◆

*I*ntimacy — or lack of it — is a big problem for me. My husband is drinking actively every day, and I have to really work my program and focus on myself to stay sane. Every day I ask my Higher Power for guidance and strength, courage and wisdom to do His will — not mine. I put my husband in God's care. I keep telling myself alcoholism is a disease, and I separate my husband from the disease.

Recently I felt very sad and depressed about my lack of intimacy. I cried and allowed myself to not follow my usual morning routine. I just didn't feel like it. Two wonderful friends from Al-Anon called me and told me just what I needed to hear: I need to feel my feelings.

Too often I stuff them, telling myself other people have problems much worse than mine, be grateful for all you have, etc. I feel so much better now, having shared my feelings with my program friends. They listen, care and understand. What a joy to belong to such a great fellowship.

I have been active in Al-Anon almost three years now. Before the program, I was a basket case — self-righteous, blaming, reacting, self-pitying, angry, resentful, miserable, and totally out of control. When I finally tried Al-Anon, it brought almost instant results for me.

I now use the Slogans and the Steps to stay on the right track. I know I can ask my Higher Power for help any time of the day or night. Working on myself is a full-time job, but the dividends in peace, serenity and freedom are worth the work.

Sexuality is one area not addressed in Al-Anon meetings and I don't know if what I'm feeling is normal or way off base. I have a four-year-old son who was born into our alcoholic home. Two years ago I hit bottom and I thought my husband had also, as he entered a treatment facility.

The months leading up to his hospitalization were a nightmare, and I certainly didn't want him to touch me or be anywhere near me. After treatment he was reluctant to initiate sex, as I was.

After a few months, the drinking and denying started again, and I made a conscious decision to stay in the marriage because divorce would mean he would have unsupervised visitation privileges. However, in my mind this was not a marriage, and I did not intend to be intimate. I did not want to live a lie. I would be polite but distant.

This philosophy usually works well — ninety percent of the time I am happy. But there are those times when I wish I could rise above the situation and be truly intimate.

At a recent Al-Anon State Convention, the speakers were all spouses of sober alcoholics. All these success stories were depressing to me. Living with an active alcoholic plus daily problems, difficulty getting to meetings due to babysitters, etc., make working my program hard — but that much more important.

My husband seems so angry at me and seldom has a kind word for me. He only drinks behind my back and would never admit it. It is hard to imagine successfully maintaining intimacy in a situation like this.

♦ ♦ ♦

In looking at the sexual and intimate aspects of my life, I had to take a look at what my needs are. I found that it's okay for me to want sex and intimacy — and that my needs are worth fulfilling. I had to come to terms with my body — how it looks, feels, etc. I had to come to terms with the fact that I am important.

I was brought up to be prim and proper. Sex and sexuality were just not discussed. I believed that wanting sex or intimacy was bad, immoral. But I'm just a normal human being with wants and needs, and I deserve to have them fulfilled. I found I was depriving myself of what little bit of intimacy I could have by my own attitudes. Once I realized these things, it became easier to be close to my husband.

Part of learning to be intimate with my husband was learning to accept him the way he is (he still drinks) — and to accept myself as a loving, warm human being with needs of my own. The Steps are the answer for me. I use the Steps and I have a sponsor who helps me look more objectively at my own behavior — not that of someone else.

When I would call my sponsor to complain that my husband wasn't home, she would say, "Take advantage of it. Do something nice for yourself."

Sometimes that meant taking the time to read and reflect. Other times it meant taking a long, hot bath or going to bed early. In this way I was able to focus on myself, and take the focus off the alcoholic.

◆ ◆ ◆

When your spouse suffers with the disease of alcoholism, even the very thought of intimacy with him can be revolting. It can actually make you physically sick (I know from experience). During my husband's active drinking years, our sexual life deteriorated to the point where I would get physically ill if he tried any intimacy at all. Yet I craved the intimacy a wife and husband should have.

The rest of our relationship was going badly, too. I finally decided it was time to end the marriage. I discussed this with my children, who listened quietly to my reasons and explanations. Then they said, "We understand, Mom. We won't be mad if you leave, but we are staying with Dad. He's sick, and he needs us."

I couldn't leave without my children, and forcing them to leave didn't seem right either. At that point, because of their feelings, I made the decision to stay.

I went back to Al-Anon meetings and to my Al-Anon literature with the determination to really work the program — to learn how to find peace and happiness for myself while honoring my commitments. My ODAT book is well worn. Some parts I know by heart.

The next ten years had ups and downs. It seemed like downs mostly, but gradually our life improved. I learned to be good to myself. Besides meetings, I took exercise classes, enrolled at a nearby junior college, learned to bowl.

I made time for my children. Besides their school activities, I was involved with their sports, my daughter's band; I was a den mother. My children and I laughed together while making good memories of baking cookies, going for walks, playing games and building snow forts. My attitude toward my husband gradually began to change.

Instead of concentrating on his faults, I looked for his good points. I followed my children's example. When he was drinking and in an ugly mood, they played quietly elsewhere. When he was sober, they interacted with him just as if he didn't have a drinking problem. They loved and respected him. They played and laughed together building more good memories; I did likewise.

On the intimacy side, I learned to be more open with my affections toward my children — hugs and kisses, saying "I love you" to them often. When my husband would allow it, I showed him the same love and affection. When he wouldn't, I would say a silent prayer to my Higher Power asking for help to make tomorrow a better day.

The first few years, there were still times of physical intimacy that were not what I would have liked. There were times when I just said no. There were times when I played chicken and avoided him. There were times when the longing for the closeness I wanted was almost overwhelming.

But gradually, this side of our marriage improved as the rest of our relationship improved. I was able to talk to him — to explain my needs, my wants, the things I would not tolerate. Eventually he was able to be more open with me.

Through the years, I would get depressed sometimes and wonder why me. Why do I always have to be the one to do the giving, the compromising, the changing? When my husband was finally able to talk about his feelings, I learned he felt the same way: he couldn't understand why I expected him to do all the compromising and changing to suit me.

Was it worth it? That talk I had with my children, when I made the decision to leave and then stay, was many years ago. My children were all under the age of ten. I now have grandchildren that age. My husband celebrated his seventeenth year of sobriety last year. Today we are the best of friends and just as romantically in love with each other as the day we got married.

♦ ♦ ♦

*I*ntimacy is a difficult issue when living with active alcoholism. Love and intimacy are lacking in my relationship with my spouse when I fail to separate him from his disease. In Al-Anon I learned how to look at my husband and how to see the disease for what it was.

For many years, I struggled with intimacy — trying to be close to him when I received only rejection and disappointment. Now I appreciate that his anger is at himself. I have been searching for my own happiness and meeting my own needs. Detaching without blame or anger is working the program and accepting the disease for what it has become.

It may happen that the relationship will not heal. Intimacy may not happen according to my wishes or desires. I may have to accept the reality of the situation. But there is always hope in Al-Anon.

♦ ♦ ♦

CHAPTER TWO

SEX AS A WEAPON

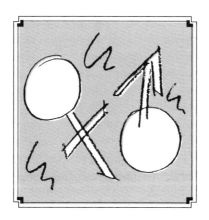

Recently, I blurted out at a meeting that I was sleeping on a small mat on the floor — luxury accommodations! My spouse was simply too drunk to even sleep with — he would toss and turn and punch me. And that was just sleeping. Sex was another matter.

The anxiety in my stomach over the drinking made it impossible for me to relax and enjoy sex. When he was drunk, I was completely turned off. He did not look like the guy I married. I couldn't trust him to be gentle and affectionate. He always seemed so rough, and he had no idea what he was doing. At times I felt he didn't even know it was me.

I reacted in a progression of ways: I tolerated it and hoped it would be over soon; I spent time in the shower; I got fat so I wouldn't turn him on; I complained of physical problems that made me unavailable. I even brought him vodka hoping he would get drunk and pass out (other times I would throw out all the liquor and beg him to stop drinking)!

Now my husband is relatively dry. I say relatively because he drinks only on special occasions. Our sex life is much better when he is dry. I haven't slept on the floor in over a year.

♦ ♦ ♦

Sex: I used and abused this side of our relationship just the same as all the other parts. I threatened with sex; I withheld sex for promises of good behavior, and I compromised myself by mistaking my motives when I used this most marvelous weapon.

How I degraded myself. I found, with hindsight, that my resentments (which manifested themselves in very ugly words and taunts) were what really drove me to the edge of insanity. I nearly lost my family as a result of this behavior.

I was so lucky to be able to talk to my very dear friends in the fellowship. I was able, a day at a time, to see my mistakes and work on them. The key to my freedom, I have found in Al-Anon, is honesty. With honesty, my Higher Power and my friends, I live and love properly today.

I have such gratitude for the loving hands that held me and

guided me through the bad times — for the people who held the principles of Al-Anon and passed them on to us (newcomers and old-timers alike) so that we could go home to bring that love to those whose lives we have affected.

♦ ♦ ♦

For the past six years, sex with my husband has been a problem for me, as his drinking (and my controlling) became worse. I came to Al-Anon just over a year ago. Somehow after several meetings, I plucked up enough courage (which must have been with the help of my Higher Power) to ask what I could do about a problem too personal to talk about in a meeting — a sex problem.

The answer I got was to call an Al-Anon member by phone or talk to someone after the meeting. So, after the meeting, someone came up to me and shared her experience, strength and hope. What we talked about changed my life.

Now my feelings toward sex and my husband have changed for the better, due to the fact that now I will only have sex with him if I feel like it, not because of fear or guilt or anything else. It is my body.

My husband doesn't always like it when I say no to him, but I am able to detach from him while letting him know that I still love him, even when I don't feel like having sex with him at the moment. I am able to tell him at the time that it's because of the way I feel, not because I am trying to punish him. When we do make love now, I can enjoy it because I know I don't have to if I don't want. My husband knows I don't like being intimate with him if he has been drinking that day or night.

I have learned that I need to show my husband compassion, not retaliation. By this I mean to make love to him when I feel like it, whether his behavior has been good or bad, because if I make love with him only when he is good, it's like he is a child and sex is his reward!

M y husband was and is an active alcoholic. Though his drinking was very controlled for the first few months of our marriage, I knew we were not like any normal newlyweds because I was always begging him for intimacy. By the time we were expecting our first child, the drinking had progressed.

Then, when I was five months pregnant, he disappeared for a few days. I was devastated. I called the Al-Anon "hotline" and spoke to someone who was willing to take me to a meeting. I walked into that meeting and, for the first time in my life, I felt like I really belonged somewhere.

After being in Al-Anon about three years, I finally realized I had to accept my husband as he was — or I had to get out of my marriage. I prayed to my Higher Power to show me His will. I was in such turmoil I could not decide if I should stay or leave.

Today we are still together and have intimacy in our relationship because I have changed. He has many good qualities, and they are where I choose to put my focus. He has a disease, and I can love him and have compassion for him. I have changed my attitudes and am minding my own business.

Thank goodness for the Serenity Prayer and my Higher Power. We are a happy family today because of those wonderful Twelve Steps. If you keep working the Al-Anon program, everything gets better in time.

◆ ◆ ◆

I 've had sex with my husband by demanding, by habit and just because it was expected. None of this was intimacy.

My sponsor shared something with me that she had heard at an Al-Anon convention: intimacy means "into-me-see." And then I went to an intimacy workshop where I heard this:

> "For a long while, I didn't want to touch my husband.
> In his early recovery I avoided him and was afraid.
> After sharing this many times at meetings and receiving
> much encouragement, I finally had the courage to go up
> to him and hug him. He grabbed me and hugged me for a
> very long time. We decided after that we would hug no
> matter what went wrong between us. Slowly intimacy

came back. My marriage is not a bed of roses, but we are on a sharing, caring basis. The journey of a thousand miles begins with one step. Al-Anon taught me to let it begin with me."

Sharings like this helped me learn to accept the disease, and meetings gave me a place to let out my anger safely. I learned that thinking, *If you would love me, there would be no conflict* was not realistic.

As I have grown in the Al-Anon program, I've realized that a relationship is what is important — and that anything after that is a bonus. If we are at war with the drinker all the time, we miss the intimacy that is there and the ways it is being shown. We need to make peace with ourselves first. Through practicing the principles of Al-Anon, I'm getting closer. After my peace with me, I need to make peace with my husband, remembering that he doesn't think the same way I do.

◆ ◆ ◆

My husband of 38 years is in the AA program, but his behavior is much the same as when he was drinking.

During the first two years of our recovery in Al-Anon and AA (the pink cloud years), we seemed to find what we both needed in our relationship despite the past indiscretions of his drinking years. Near the end of those years, however, I realized I was again a doormat. He was using me to fulfill his needs, and mine were of little importance to him.

Open and positive conversations regarding the intimacy I needed were quickly ended by him without an offer or suggestion of working together to improve our intimacy — physical or emotional.

The First Step reminded me I was — and am — powerless over the disease. At times, this is very hard to accept. The past two years have been extremely difficult because of my determination to work my program and live my life. His unacceptable behavior has caused problems within the family as well as in our relationship.

The intimacy between me and my husband has ended — my

choice. What I still have is my Higher Power and the Al-Anon program, which have given me sanity, serenity and the freedom to live one day at a time.

◆ ◆ ◆

I don't know how common this problem is in other alcoholic marriages, but my husband's sexual rejection of me was overwhelming. He would become very interested in sex for a couple of nights — and then have absolutely no desire for several weeks, usually months, even up to a year.

He has repeatedly explained to me that his lack of desire has nothing to do with me and that I am indeed attractive to him. His problem is a symptom of his illness and his depression. But that's been very hard for me to accept, and through our six years of marriage, I have wasted many hours crying, explaining, begging and nagging. It is possible that the psychiatric help my husband is receiving can help him change — but I have finally accepted that I cannot change him.

Through Al-Anon I have learned to make every other area of my life as fulfilling as I possibly can. I find fulfillment in my friendships, my job, my relationship with the Higher Power, my crafts and my music. I am learning to feel good about myself.

Secondly, I am learning to accept reality. He has a problem. My strong desire for a sexual relationship is normal. I'm okay: it's all right to feel frustrated about it.

When I feel my frustration starting to dominate my thoughts, I deliberately turn to some activity that will help me change that and make me feel glad to be alive. I go shopping, read a book, or go roller skating with a friend. If I don't do something, I become depressed and unbearable to live with — for my husband and, more importantly, for me.

So I make sure I get plenty of sleep. I can handle my emotions better when I'm rested. I take care of myself physically. I dress well, I work at being well-groomed. I exercise, eat right and wear a pleasant expression.

I've stopped trying to figure out why my husband is the way

he is. Further analyzing of the problem wastes my valuable time
and becomes a good excuse to feel sorry for myself.

Perspective is essential for me. Our sexual relationship is only
one area of my life. I'm not saying this is an easy situation to
accept, but my changed attitudes and actions make it a lot easier.

◆ ◆ ◆

My husband's alcoholism did not become apparent until we
had been married about ten years. I had not recognized it
as alcoholism, but the drinking was always a problem for me.
By that time, we had three children.

I thought about leaving each time a crisis arose, but I never
threatened to leave because I knew I would never follow
through. My conscious reason was that our children needed their
father — and it was true. They obviously loved him and he
them. He wasn't a perfect father — but I wasn't a perfect mother
either. We each gave the best in us to our children.

That was my conscious reason. I did not find the other reasons until I had been in Al-Anon for a number of years and began to realize that our sex life had not been successful from the
very beginning. That is not to say it was not tolerable or in
some ways pleasurable. Over the years it stayed the same —
never improving, never becoming any worse.

When he was about fifty-five years old, my husband decided
on his own that he wanted nothing more to do with sex. I felt
dumped. I reasoned I had gone along with sex as he presented it
for twenty years — why couldn't he try to accept me? We never
talked about sex, so when he decided to give it up, he didn't tell
me. Today I believe his alcoholism made sex impossible for him,
but at the time, I felt bitter and angry and our relationship began to come apart.

I didn't leave even then. I was dependent in every way —
financially and emotionally. I feared leaving the security of my
home. I feared trying to make it on my own.

I carried resentments against him for many years. When he
became sober and began going to AA meetings, I went to

Al-Anon because it was strongly recommended. When I finally recognized my recovery depended on accepting help from my Higher Power, and that a sponsor could help me to understand the program, I slowly began to give up my various resentments.

Resentment about sex was the last to go. Today at seventy, I still have a desire for sex — but I have been able to accept what I cannot change. I have also learned that I hold the keys to my own happiness or misery. Those realizations gave me the freedom to be me. I still live with my husband, and he is still sober. His sexual desires did not return with his sobriety nine years ago.

I have come to realize that no one has everything they want in life, and I have been able to let go of that over which I have no control. Maintaining my own happiness and attending to problems that are mine to solve has been the answer for me. I live a fruitful and productive life, and I believe the Al-Anon program helps each one of us do that in a highly individual way.

CHAPTER THREE

BAD DAYS MADE BETTER

My husband is an active alcoholic in denial about the disease. He doesn't verbally communicate with me except for small talk, and he never reaches out to me or touches me in any way at all. I learned to cope by not thinking about it. We both work, and he is out of the house by the time I wake up. In the evening, we spend one or two hours in each other's company. We have our meal together and he retires directly. I go to bed about an hour later and he is already asleep. I usually slip into our bed with him, but if he has been drinking too much and smells badly, I sleep in the guest room.

He pays the bills; he lets me do what I find fulfilling. I fill my time and life with my God, my grown children, other family members, friends, my job and Al-Anon. Going to a psychologist is very helpful to me. I also treat myself to a massage every two weeks. It is a super-relaxing hour where I truly unwind and enjoy.

I'm a hugger — a friendly, cheerful person. I don't feel I'm living a terribly deprived existence under the present circumstances, but I know it could be better. I believe if I keep in touch with myself, bravely face what I can change and leave the rest to God, it will get better sooner or later.

◆ ◆ ◆

My husband and I have a strong marriage, good communication, adequate sex, 17 years of AA and 15 years of Al-Anon. But, usually, any concern or solicitude proffered is in the nature of a trade-off for intimacy. That's not all bad. Many, I know, don't even have that. But I need closeness with *no strings* attached, and I have learned to take it in other ways — where and when it comes:

- My present sponsor is a caring person.

- My home group has sensitive, loving people.

- We do a lot of hugging and calling each other on the phone.

It has been necessary for me to learn two things. First, that gentleness and affection are totally and completely possible emotions without any hint of sexual overtones. And second, that I must not reject warmth just because it is not coming from the source I may expect.

All living creatures need nurturing and I'm no exception. Al-Anon gives me a new chance. It offers me opportunities to have my needs met in new ways. I can love without expecting to be loved back, and I can express my love for others openly, with a freedom I never believed possible.

I was raised by a mother who was too busy reacting to living with an alcoholic to have any capacity for demonstrative fondness. I believe that my husband would, if he could, be cherishing today. But he can't — and that's that.

♦ ♦ ♦

Alcohol kills love. I had to relearn to care for my husband. One suggestion from Al-Anon was to look at the alcoholic when he didn't know I was looking, and repeat to myself over and over again, *I love you*. This is the way it started.

I'm doing better about not expecting too much. As for sex, we went from none to once in awhile, and sometimes I feel comfortable about initiating it. We now enjoy each other's company — not all the time — but more than in the past. I've learned that, although today we have a good time together, tomorrow might not be the same.

My Al-Anon meetings help. Being around people who are trying to improve their life (and who are in the same situation I am) means a lot.

♦ ♦ ♦

During the period of my husband's active drinking, he would be out for days. When he returned, he could not remember where he had been. Sometimes, even in the midst of such insanity, we still felt love and the need to show it. However, I had to think about the possibility that he might be carrying a disease, which was a realistic possibility.

Through Al-Anon, I realized I was faced with a serious decision. Alcoholism affects every facet of our lives, but with the help of our Higher Power and our Al-Anon meetings, we can get through most anything, one day at a time.

After a few more binges, my husband got a complete physical. I believe that was the beginning of his recovery. It took almost a year for me to be truly comfortable in our intimate relationship.

Al-Anon has taught me to be responsible for myself and to allow him to be responsible for himself.

♦ ♦ ♦

M y husband and I were married after I'd been in Al-Anon eight months. During that time our sex life was just great. Immediately after the ceremony, however, it seemed sex had been chopped clear out of our lives. I thought the man I had fallen in love with had been left at the ceremony. I thought I was going crazy. I would reach out to him, and I'd get a very negative response. Three or four times a week became once or twice a month. I became frantic. Fortunately I kept going to Al-Anon.

Al-Anon gave me alternatives. I learned to deal with my resentments, and I gained the courage to speak out about my discomfort. I was able to talk quietly without raising my voice.

The problem hasn't improved much, but my attitude has — because of the Steps, the Slogans and love from my sponsors. I have received a gift from Al-Anon: freedom. Freedom to accept my spouse as an individual with his own problems and hangups. Now sex is fine, though infrequent.

The reason I can and do tolerate this is because life with my actively drinking spouse has good days that are so good they make the bad days better.

♦ ♦ ♦

I t is often a great relief to many of us to find that the sexual problems we had been experiencing have also been experienced by others in Al-Anon. It takes courage for many of us to approach this still taboo subject, and people often find it hard to speak openly about it.

When I came to Al-Anon, I was allowing my husband to

help himself to me on a regular basis. I was unable to say no. I don't know whether this was because I feared he would leave me, or because I feared his anger and his rejection, or because I was just incapable of saying the word. In any case, I did not have enough self-worth or respect for my body to do what I wanted.

Eventually I split up with my husband and entered a relationship with someone else. To my dismay, I found I was again unable to cope with the sexual side of the relationship, which had initially been good. This time I just had to look at me. With the gentle help of my sponsor, I was able to see that I had grown up with a badly recorded message about sex. By inference, my parents had let me know sex was naughty and dirty, and my first sexual experiences confirmed this for me. I started to use sex as a rebellion against them. I also used it as something to hide behind, something to ensure I got attention, something with which to get affection (albeit transient).

When I stopped and looked, I realized that I was petrified not only of sex, but of being close to anyone. This fear of intimacy made me destroy relationships before they had begun. The risk of someone getting too close to me was something I couldn't entertain, because if they saw me as I really was, they would reject me. I had built my whole personality around a very flirtatious, sexual persona — but I was actually frightened of sex.

Today I have a wonderful relationship. I will say no for weeks at a time if that is what is right for me. I have sex only when I want to, not to *people please* someone else. It is my body, and the only person who has the right to take pleasure from it is myself. I am not frightened of sex anymore.

◆ ◆ ◆

My husband is an active alcoholic. We have been married for twenty-two years, and for most of that time have enjoyed our sexual relationship. He is a gentle, caring man — not violent or abusive.

However, his excessive drinking has affected his health over the years. During the last few years, his performance has dwindled down to the sorry state that he is now unable to perform at all. This is a great disappointment to me. Most of the time I can accept switching off my feelings, though there are times when I long for intimacy.

I have asked myself why I stay in the marriage. Is it my deeply rooted attitude that marriage is synonymous with *til death us do part*? Or does it haunt me that a marriage break-up would confirm my long-held belief that I am a failure?

I'm still on the road of self-discovery in Al-Anon. I have learned that my worst moments are when I allow negative thinking to creep in and when I let self-pity rear its ugly head. With God's help, I am living the program a day at a time. Maybe this, too, shall pass.

Because I love my husband, I show my love for him by the care I take to cook his meals, wash his clothes and be pleasant most times. I touch him as I pass, or smile a greeting when he comes home weary from work. I don't always feel love for him when he delays a meal while he consumes liquor, or when he stays in bed all day on a holiday, or when he refuses to accompany me someplace. Awareness that God doesn't always give us what we want, but always gives us what we need, has helped me.

◆ ◆ ◆

I had been in the program about eight years before I started looking honestly at my relationship with my sober, alcoholic spouse. Though I realized things were not well, I was completely unprepared for what I was to find.

I knew in my heart things were not right. Sexually I wasn't interested — and neither was he. I felt I was a *front* for him, a show of marriage. As I delved into exploring the relationship, pieces of the past fit the puzzle. Finally, he admitted he had a homosexual past. My world was shattered.

Without the program, I do not know how I would have reacted to learning, after 20 years and four children, that I had married a homosexual. Al-Anon helped me learn to accept the situation. I did not cause the problem. He chose to come out of the closet, and I did file for separation. Finally, we were divorced.

My attorney was amazed at how accepting I was — and surprised I was not a basket case. I pointed out that Al-Anon was a
lifesaver for me.

Today I continue to attend my Al-Anon meetings because I
want and need them. There is a correlation between my clear
thinking and my attendance at meetings. The children and I
have a good relationship; I have joined some singles' groups and
am meeting some nice people. I'm scared at times, but I know
with God's help, I'll be all right. Life is good with God.

♦ ♦ ♦

One thing Al-Anon has given me is freedom — freedom from
worrying about normalcy, freedom to leave or stay with the
alcoholic, to have sex or not have sex with the alcoholic, to
change the things I can — or not change anything for now. The
ball was in my court once I found Al-Anon.

Today I live with an active alcoholic — one who'd had success
in AA but then later fell away. Before AA I treated him like a
wayward brother. And you don't sleep with your brother.

Then came decision time when the wayward brother turned
into the husband. How could I turn emotions on and off? I have
found the golden rule works wonders. Please him and he'll
please you. Let go and let God love him through you. A doormat no, but a welcome mat yes!

CHAPTER FOUR

IT TAKES TWO

*F*or the longest time, sex in my life referred to gender, certainly not to an act of love between husband and wife. I constantly told my husband I was frustrated. Yet when he did turn towards me, I would reject him with the kind of remarks that would have made the most potent of men impotent.

I used my frustration as energy — angry energy. I cleaned house like a maniac. Everything had to be my way. And I was never satisfied. Now I know that all I wanted was to be loved — but without being loving. How can any man be loving to a wife who is always berating him or screaming *love me*!

My pride and moral standards would not allow me to turn elsewhere for physical satisfaction. I didn't want anyone to know that my life wasn't the way I led people to believe it was.

My husband and I each found our programs three years ago, and our life is getting better. I don't clean like a maniac any-more. Our sex life wouldn't compare to the great lovers, but it is satisfying and loving — even fun!

Through Al-Anon, I have become more sure of my own worth and no longer feel lonely and unloved as I once did. I have also come to learn that love is an attitude in my life that I don't have to prove or have proven to me. My husband has always been undemonstrative, and I can accept that now. A pat on the fanny is his way of saying *I love you*.

Last August was our 30th anniversary — we reaffirmed our wedding vows. When I made my vow to him, I meant it with all my heart.

◆ ◆ ◆

*W*hen I could not honestly and comfortably respond to my husband sexually, instead of refusing him I would postpone. I would say one of the following in a non-critical, non-condemn-ing manner, keeping my voice under control:

- Let's wait until morning.
- I'll make a date with you for tomorrow night.
- Can you wait until tomorrow?
- Could we wait until tomorrow?

*H*aving spent many years in an alcoholic relationship, my self-esteem and self-worth went way down. One of the major areas affected was my sex life. I am admitting this for the first time, having been in Al-Anon for two years.

I am now in a relationship with somebody who is also in a Twelve-Step program. Through the help of my Higher Power and the Al-Anon program, I know I can face this problem; I am not alone.

I love my partner and want to be able to have a fulfilled relationship with him. The feeling of being used is slowly leaving me. I know the problem is with me and my attitudes. The courage to change the things I can is what I am working on — one day at a time.

◆ ◆ ◆

I am very grateful to some members of Al-Anon I once heard speaking, in an open way, about their sexual feelings. Their sharings helped me to take an honest look at myself. Before that, I had not dealt with the way I had handled sex from about the age of 16 until the time I got married.

Sex used to happen to me. Some guy would start chatting me up, and we would end up having sex together. I rarely had a loving relationship with anyone.

All this hopping into bed stopped when I met my husband, who insisted on faithfulness (for which I am grateful now). I remember being at a dinner party, where I kept looking at one of the men over and over again. I was quite upset when I caught myself doing it.

From that recent experience, I know that a lot of sick thinking and reacting is still with me. I know today that I was a very sick person before I married the alcoholic, and the way I used to handle sex was part of that sickness.

After ten months of sobriety, my husband and I separated. It was only afterwards that I could begin to see where I had failed to contribute to our marriage.

I complained when he made excuses not to be home, but I never gave him any reason to want to stay home. I wanted to be loved, but was unloving. I wanted consideration, but was inconsiderate. I wanted respect, but showed him none. I wanted him to listen and to understand, but turned him off. I wanted freedom to find myself and develop new interests, but resented him for wanting the same.

After two months, we decided to try again. We needed that separation to learn to grow separately so we could begin to grow together.

◆ ◆ ◆

I used to enjoy sex with my husband, but I also used to drink with him. Gradually, as drinking became less important to me, I began to realize that when he was drunk, he showed little or no consideration for me. I lived with that for awhile before our sex life went downhill.

Now I've found Al-Anon, and through the program I am learning where I've made mistakes. I'd always blamed the problem on my husband, but it really was partly my fault. It was the way I reacted to him. I tried to protect him for fear of hurting him. I allowed him to put guilt and pressure on me to perform. I was so afraid he would leave me that I hid the truth.

Lately I've been doing a lot of Fourth-Step work on the problem of sex — and I'm getting somewhere.

◆ ◆ ◆

My husband and I had never been very close. He was a loner — a married bachelor. At first his business kept him away from home for long hours; then drinking at bars filled his evenings. As the years went by, he became more and more of a free agent. He never told me where he was staying when he went away on business trips. Where he went (and what he did) were his business.

Several times while he'd been drinking, I'd become aware that he had engaged in extramarital sex, but I just cried by myself and lived with it. When he stopped drinking, I hoped this behavior would stop, but I never mentioned it.

Finally we did talk about it, and he proposed that we continue to live as we had — married, but with him free to do as he chose. That was unacceptable to me. He moved out, but did agree to go once to a marriage counselor. From that one traumatic meeting, he agreed to yet another session — and then to a few more. This continued for two months.

The fault is never one-sided. I had contributed my share. My hurt and resentment had come out vindictively. I had become utterly passive during lovemaking. Now I faced this truth. I sought all the help I could: Al-Anon meetings, talks with my sponsor, a talk with her pastor and mine.

I spent a lot of time with my Higher Power reading and meditating. Let me tell you, I did a lot of thrashing around — but to get peace, I had to release my husband, our marriage and everything that went with it. In the midst of all this, there were many little blessings, but the big blessing was facing the problem, facing myself in all my ugliness, and (while not liking it) accepting what had been and what was.

After two months we decided to try again. There were no promises, but my husband showed a sincere desire to work out his problem, and I worked on mine.

It has been a year since then. Several months ago, my husband casually mentioned that he hasn't had any of those old problems, that I don't have to worry about it anymore. Our relationship is far from perfect, but it continues to grow. I am thankful that we are still together and that we can continue to change.

My marriage is just over eight years old. Of these years, only seven months were shared with an active drinker. The remaining years have been shared with a man struggling for (and achieving) sobriety.

Since I am now 56, it follows that I was no chicken when I embarked into this partnership. My eyes were wide open; I was going to be the necessary cure-all! At the age of 48, I imagined myself to be reasonably mature, yet I did not recognize alcoholism for what it was. In just a few short months, my husband was in the throes of the DTs and severe withdrawal symptoms, which were almost fatal despite medical care and hospitalization.

All that has been achieved since then adds up to this: I am now able to say that I am maturing — a day at a time — the Al-Anon way, just as he says he is recovering a day at a time. Sobriety brings differing problems to differing people. No marriage is without some ups and downs, surely. Al-Anon has taught me to not lay blame for these at the alcoholic's feet.

One thing I have learned: those nearest to recovering alcoholics are often those with whom they find communication most difficult. Showing affection is often difficult for our partners. But it is there, and I've learned to value it in little things — not just in physical ways. Today I believe that a good marriage is one in which two people don't only enjoy things together (though this is good), but one in which two people can endure things together. Al-Anon has taught me this, and I am truly grateful.

♦ ♦ ♦

CHAPTER FIVE

NEW CLOSENESS

*I*need a lot of sexual love and caring, and I decided that if I
gave my touching, love and care to my husband, I would get
the same back. I didn't. This made me frustrated, confused —
and I went into a depression.

Through Al-Anon, I began to realize what the problem was.
My husband told me if I gave him some space to come around
me, I wouldn't be so unhappy. He said I gave my love and care
to him, but that if I didn't get the same in return, I would look
like a lost puppy.

I stopped giving so much and let him take the initiative. Then
I did receive the love and caring I needed. My expectations had
been too great for him. When he could tell me this in so many
words, I then searched myself more deeply. I'm going to work on
just me for a while.

♦ ♦ ♦

*H*onesty to me means that it's time to look at me. Am I sharing my true feelings, even at the risk of rejection? Am I fear-
ful that my spouse and friends won't like me or accept me as I
am?

I used to think that being in Al-Anon meant I was supposed
to be in control of my emotions at all times. I have found it is
normal to get angry. It's okay to be hurt when someone says
something hurtful to me.

I had to start with feelings of guilt, anger, jealousy — look at
them, accept and forgive myself. I had to deal with fear in
telling my spouse what I think a relationship is. I had to learn
to share my feelings about our sex life. I had to risk the fear of
rejection.

To do this, I had to turn to my Higher Power. I had to have
faith that, if it was meant for us to be together, then God would
give us the ability to understand and accept each other. If we
couldn't, then we really didn't have a sharing relationship — it
was built only on sex.

Sex is an important part of love and marriage, but not the
principal one. What's basic is caring, sharing and accepting each
other as human beings who make mistakes, can admit them
and forgive each other.

Sometimes it seemed I was the one who had to set the guide-lines for our marriage. I felt I was beating my head against the wall. I could keep cool by using the Steps, the Slogans, and mostly my Higher Power to figure out what I wanted from my life and my marriage.

I knew that I did love my husband, although I didn't always like what he did or how he treated me. I had allowed this dur-ing early sobriety because of fears of rocking the boat or losing him. Then I realized again that my feelings could not get him drunk, only his wanting to drink could do that.

I have also had to take a look at my ability to accept his feel-ings without anger, resentment or hurt. He has never shared with anyone. He is just as frail as I am. I have had to take the time to listen and think a lot about what he is saying without reacting immediately — especially if it is a feeling that he is sharing.

This has been one of the most beautiful experiences I have ever had. It's like a rose unfolding — with dew drops falling down the petals. Al-Anon is not easy, but using its principles and the Higher Power, I have found it is simple. Also, I am mar-ried one day at a time. This simplifies my life.

◆ ◆ ◆

Yes it is possible to have sex with an active alcoholic. Having sexual desires and human needs for intimacy with my less-than-perfect mate tells me there is more to our relationship than convenience and parenthood. There are very deep currents of love and enjoyment buried under years of misunderstanding, pain, anger and hate.

Sometimes my surrender to him and to my own needs helps pave the way for kindness, respect and regard. I can surrender — not to my husband, but to God — even in the sexual act of sur-render. I can surrender to my own emotions and physical needs. They are real, and the path to fulfilling them is my way of ac-knowledging them, affirming myself.

Giving both of us the pleasure and reassurance of sex helps break down the walls we have built between each other. When

I accept the reality of my marriage to another imperfect human being, I grow closer to God. I grow from acknowledging my full humanity and my husband's right to be as broken as he is and still be lovable.

My husband has worked hard to change himself — and I have continued to work my program. We have passed through some crises that came close to ending our marriage and are both much better for having come through them. This program works, and my family situation improves as I apply its principles in my life.

♦ ♦ ♦

I felt I was too young to give up the physical side of marriage. My husband went from the world's greatest lover to a ten-year period of abstinence. After a few failed attempts at lovemaking while sober, apparently his ego wouldn't let him try again.

Talking with other women in the program didn't begin to fill the void. A long-time male member recommended I read AA's Big Book. From that I gained the strength to accept what I couldn't change, the courage to change my attitude, and the wisdom to realize we are imperfect people living in an imperfect world. Expectations of having the perfect marriage had robbed me of my serenity.

Shortly after I turned my husband over to God, he suffered a near-fatal heart attack. For the first time in over a decade, I heard *I love you* from his lips when he hadn't been drinking.

That was when I learned that sex is only one part of intimacy — that intimacy encompasses caring and sharing, laughing, crying and praying together, touching and hugging, giving and taking. This is true intimacy.

After a few months, he took up his old habits again. In the past, I detached with indifference and sometimes hate. My detaching is now done with love. Today I am married to an active alcoholic who may or may not come home drunk tonight. Today I have taken care of my responsibilities, done something nice for someone else, and something good for me. Today I have had a successful day.

*T*oday my husband and I have a good relationship, including emotional as well as physical intimacy. We must work to maintain it, but the benefits are more than worth the extra energy. It takes more than energy for me to maintain a cold distance from someone I love.

Al-Anon taught me to not blame others for my own unhappiness. I can't do anything about someone else's actions, but I can do something about my own. When I honestly looked at my part in our relationship, I was surprised to see how much I contributed to our problems. This humbled me into realizing that I don't have all the answers.

I began to work on my own attitude. I learned to detach from him when his behavior was inappropriate, but enjoy him when he was sober. As I worked my program, I saw that I was treating him a lot like he was treating me. I then tried to treat him as I wanted to be treated. Whenever possible, compliments and encouragement replaced criticism. Respect replaced disgust. Love and understanding replaced anger. Quiet statements replaced loud arguments. I realized he is doing the best he can. This helped me to stop expecting and start accepting.

Today things are not perfect between us, but I have learned to accept and appreciate what we do have. It is in the atmosphere of acceptance that intimacy develops. I am grateful for the tools of Al-Anon, among them detachment, sponsorship, working on myself, and putting the alcoholic into God's hands.

◆ ◆ ◆

*M*y beloved husband, who is now deceased due to lung cancer, was a very beautiful man. But he didn't become that way overnight. It took several years in the AA program.

My husband became sober shortly after I went into Al-Anon. I expected an instant Cary Grant or Don Juan for sure. I even considered a divorce because he attended meetings constantly and I was lonesome for his attention.

Little by little, it dawned on me that this dear man was getting a lousy deal: the only love I showed him had strings attached. It was time for me to grow up and do my share by becoming a loving wife.

I started by being a little more considerate about TV programs, about timing my questions, about stating my feelings. It was difficult, but Al-Anon told me I could say anything to anyone as long as I remained calm, loving, and didn't go on too long. I told him: "I love you, and I get lonesome for some of your time." I told him, "Let's go out to dinner." I told him, "Let's go to a meeting together."

We started listening to each other's feelings without judging. Our love grew and grew. We shared a most beautiful, loving sex life. We shared program language. We both realized the best gift we could give our four children was learning to love one another.

I want to emphasize that it takes time. I said many, many prayers asking God to teach me how to reach out in love.

Then, about three years ago, my husband developed lung cancer and it was terminal. He was given a few years to live. He and I grew closer than I ever dreamed possible — sharing the load, learning acceptance, and living in today.

We enjoyed a very active life. We were given the privilege of speaking together at Al-Anon and AA programs (sometimes our four children joined us). Together we shared our love for the fellowship and the program.

When Bob died, he left a legacy of faith, hope, love and courage that's a part of all five of us today.

◆ ◆ ◆

Few people are comfortable discussing their sex lives in public, yet one night there I was at an Al-Anon meeting where the question was, "Is sex a natural expression of your love?" I answered painfully and truthfully. "No. No it isn't. Not a bit!"

That experience was very helpful. Afterwards, some of the long-time members were able to reassure me that almost everyone who is involved in an alcoholic marriage has some sort of difficulty in the realm of sex — that there was not necessarily something wrong with me.

The timing of this discussion was ironic because, the night before, my husband and I had experienced real disappointment in our physical relationship. I had always considered myself an ardent person. But gradually, in our three years of marriage, I had become less and less responsive to my husband.

Looking back, I can see that before Al-Anon, I used to believe all his critical remarks about me. I accepted his destructive criticism, not realizing it was the distortion of a pained mind and a tortured soul. The sexually oriented remarks were the ones that hurt the most. I became convinced that I was inadequate — as friend, as wife, as lover.

In Al-Anon, I learned to detach, to begin to let go and let God. I also began to develop a life of my own and grow as a person. I began to treat my husband with greater courtesy and warmth, and I no longer listened to his criticism of me if he was drinking. I ceased to be a doormat.

Gradually our life together improved. Within a period of a few months, we were able to be friends again. The senseless arguments stopped. Everything improved — except our sex life.

Despite sincere discussions in non-drinking moments, I was totally unable to respond with enthusiasm. The word "frigid" began to be used. As my husband's sense of frustration grew, so did my sense of inadequacy.

As for many others, God and sex had never been closely associated in my mind — just the opposite, to be truthful. I began to put myself into God's hands while lying next to my husband. My hope was that if I were a little calmer, things might improve. And they did.

Soon I was able to tolerate my husband's caresses, and as I continued to let go and let God, I was able to respond with increasing ardor — so much so that my husband asked me what had brought about the change.

I am profoundly grateful for the new closeness we have been able to share. There are times when actions speak louder than words, and sexual contact can be a powerful source of healing and unity.

*T*he alcoholic I live with had been in AA for three years before I finally saw the light from under the Al-Anon door. That light saved my life and kept our marriage together.

With the help of our programs, we finally began to communicate, to laugh, to enjoy each other again. However, one obstacle remained: intimacy.

Somewhere inside I felt the need for intimacy, but had an overwhelming fear of making the first move. After all this time of doing my best to abstain, how could I work my way into feeling comfortable again?

Everything else was on the mend. Why did sex have to be so important? I wished our friendship would be enough. And I became willing to settle for this.

I used the Slogans *Let Go and Let God* and *One Day At A Time.* These told me that my Higher Power would remove my fears while I tried to show love to my husband in easier ways. The little things, like acknowledging touches and warm smiles. Gradually, these *little things* grew into hugs and kisses — and saying *I love you* before he did. Eventually I was able to make love with a little more ease (and a little less fantasy).

It's a slow process, just like my program. But it's working and it's freeing — and we are together again.

After all this time of trying to figure out why I love him, now I'm learning. He's been so patient with me. You know, I even think he'd rather have the hugs and kisses and touches than anything else. Now he knows he's loved.